# Encouraging Words
## for a
# Woman After God's Own Heart®

# Elizabeth George

*Paintings by* Judy Buswell

## HARVEST HOUSE PUBLISHERS
### EUGENE, OREGON

# Encouraging Words for A Woman After God's Own Heart®

Text Copyright © 2004 by Elizabeth George
Published by Harvest House Publishers
Eugene, Oregon 97402
www.harvesthousepublishers.com

For more information regarding the author of this book, please contact:
Elizabeth George
P.O. Box 2879
Belfair, WA 98528
1-800-542-4611
www.elizabethgeorge.com

Library of Congress Cataloging-in-Publication Data

George, Elizabeth, 1944-
  Encouraging words for a woman after God's own heart / Elizabeth George;
paintings by Judy Buswell.
      p. cm.
A collection of inspiring stories and original prayers from the author's
A woman after God's own heart and A woman's high calling. Includes
bibliographical references.
    ISBN 0-7369-1172-3 (alk. paper)
  1. Christian women--Prayer-books and devotions--English. 2. Christian
women--Religious life. I. George, Elizabeth, 1944- Woman after God's
own heart. II. George, Elizabeth, 1944-   . Woman's high calling. III.
Title.
    BV4844.G42 2004
    242'.643--dc22
                              2003015296

All works of art reproduced in this book are copyrighted by Judy Buswell and licensed
by MHS Licensing, Minneapolis, Minnesota, and may not be reproduced without
permission.

Design and production by Garborg Design Works, Minneapolis, Minnesota

Harvest House Publishers, Inc. is the exclusive licensee of the federally registered
trademark, A WOMAN AFTER GOD'S OWN HEART.

Portions of this text have previously appeared in *A Woman After God's Own Heart*® by
Elizabeth George (Harvest House Publishers, 1997) and *A Woman's High Calling* by
Elizabeth George (Harvest House Publishers, 2001).

**Printed in China**

04  05  06  07  08  09  10  11  12  13  / LP /  10  9  8  7  6  5  4  3  2  1

# Contents

# Encouraging Words for Your Heart

*Love the Lord your God
with all your heart and
with all your soul and
with all your strength and
with all your mind....*

—LUKE 10:27

# Making Every Minute Count

*But only one thing is needed.*
*Mary has chosen what is better,*
*and it will not be taken away from her.*

—LUKE 10:42

*I* had done it thousands of times before, but two days ago it was different. I'm talking about the walk I take each day in the dewy part of the morning. As I moved through my neighborhood I noticed a woman—probably in her late seventies—walking on the sidewalk by the park. She had an aluminum walker and appeared to have suffered a stroke. She was also a little bent over, a telltale sign of osteoporosis.

What made this outing different for me? Well, just three days earlier we had buried my husband's mother. Lois was in her late seventies when God called her home to be with Him...and Lois had used an aluminum walker...and Lois had suffered from osteoporosis...and Lois, too, had experienced a slight stroke. Still grieving over our recent loss, I was a little down even before I spotted this woman who so reminded me of Lois.

As I watched that dear, brave woman struggling to walk and remembered Lois's battle with cancer and pneumonia at the end of her life, I realized that I was taking a hard look at reality. Every one of us has a body that will someday fail us—and that "someday" is not necessarily too far off. I was also sharply reminded once again of how desperately I want my life—indeed each and every day of it, each and every minute of it—to count.

Dear one, I know you want the same thing. And here's hope and comfort—Lois was a woman after God's own heart. She chose the good part, which shall never be taken away. She chose to live every day for God. She loved God, worshiped God, walked with God, served God. She shows us how important it is to choose to love God and follow after Him…with a whole heart…each day…as long as we live. Every day—and every minute—counts when we are devoted to God.

*Father of all life…*
*Thank You for each fresh new day.*
*Help me to live each minute*
*with a heart devoted to You.*

# Our Recipe for Godliness

*Pursue righteousness, godliness,*
*faith, love, endurance and gentleness.*

—1 TIMOTHY 6:11

*W*atching my daughters grow into responsible
women has been a constant delight to me as a
mother. Now that they've become adults and ventured out
on their own, I hope and pray that I've given them enough
of the basics to build their lives on—the basics of the
Christian faith, the basics of homemaking, and the basics
of cooking. One night, though, I wasn't so sure.

For several years Katherine enjoyed the fun and fellow-
ship of sharing an apartment with some other young

women from our church. Part of the adventure was cooking for the group on her assigned nights. But when she began to date her Paul, the two of them spent many an evening at our home "hanging out" with Jim and me. On one of those nights Katherine decided to dig out our smudged old recipe—a long-time family favorite—and bake some brownies to top off our evening. Because I don't normally make them for just Jim and me, we could hardly wait for those brownies to cool down enough to eat them with tall glasses of cold milk!

Finally we each had a huge, warm brownie to bite into—but after one taste we knew we wouldn't be taking a second bite. Something was missing. Not wanting to hurt Katherine's feelings, we took turns mumbling something somewhat kind like "Hmmm, these taste different..." or "Hmmm, they sure do *smell* good..." and "Oh, Kath, thanks for making us brownies." Finally I asked her if she might have left anything out. With all the gusto in the world, she cheerfully volunteered, "Oh, yes, I left out the salt! At the apartment I've been learning to cook without salt. Salt's bad for us." Those brownies had to be thrown out because a single missing ingredient—a little teaspoon of salt—kept them from being edible.

Just as a batch of brownies requires several ingredients to become what we intend it to be, several ingredients are key to us becoming a woman after God's own heart, ingredients like devotion to God, devotion to His Word, and devotion to prayer. But there is one more ingredient—as important as salt in brownies—that goes into making you and me spiritually complete, and that is obedience. The heart God delights in is a heart that is compliant, cooperative, and responsive to Him and His commands, a heart that obeys. This, dear friend, is our recipe for godliness.

*Father of all righteousness...*
*Thank You that You have revealed in Your Word*
*Your good and acceptable and perfect will for my life.*
*Help me to follow after You and Your will*
*with my whole heart.*

# Our Source of Peace

*You will keep him in perfect peace,*
*whose mind is stayed on You,*
*because he trusts in You.*

—Isaiah 26:3 (NKJV)

My mind is reflecting back to a day when Jim and I were visiting our daughter Courtney and her children. Her Paul had just left on his first-ever submarine tour…for 90 days! Jim and I were there to sort of ease the shock and help fill the void such an assignment from the U.S. Navy was bound to create.

All was going well—in fact, better than any of us had anticipated. So Jim and I decided to run some errands to bring some things home for all of us. We told Courtney not to hold lunch for us, but to just go right ahead and we would see her when we got back. And off we went.

We came back to Courtney's house at about 2:00 and

headed up the stairs, turned the corner, and there she was (or, should I say, there *it* was?!). Courtney was sitting in her rocking chair with her feet up on an ottoman. She had a blanket draped over her legs. Her Bible was open on her lap. But that's not the half of it. The dining room, I have to report, looked like a bomb had gone off! The floor was trashed. The table was covered and smeared with food and spilled milk. I maybe even spotted some spaghetti noodles hanging from the light fixture overhead and drooping off the backs of the chairs! The whole scene resembled a war zone.

Jim and I looked at the damage...and we looked at Courtney. And then she said, "You won't believe all that happened here after you left. I was just sitting here trying to calm down and asking God to remind me of how much I love and wanted these children."

I personally think that my daughter found a fine solution that particular day to her real-life situation as a mother. She had the grace to know that her spiritual needs at that moment came first. And she had the sense (again, thanks to God's grace) to just stop, leave things as they were, and look to the Lord for His patience, His peace, and a quiet spirit. I have to say I was very Christian-proud of Courtney that day. It appeared that she had "got it" in her understanding of God's plan and role for her as a Christian mother.

*Father of all peace...*
*Thank You for Your peace that passes*
*all understanding...and misunderstanding!*
*Help me to steadfastly trust You in all things.*

# Filled and Overflowing

*May the God of hope fill you
with all joy and peace as you trust in him,
so that you may overflow with hope
by the power of the Holy Spirit.*

—ROMANS 15:13

Have you ever heard about the "Seven Sacred Pools" on the island of Maui, Hawaii? I was privileged to see them for myself on a family trip. These breathtaking pools have been formed in the rocks and lava beds by rain rushing down the mountainsides toward the Pacific Ocean. Originating high above in altitudes unseen because of the ever-present rain clouds, the fresh water falls to the ground, first filling the highest pool. When that top pool is full, the still-falling rain causes its contents to overflow and cascade into another pool down the mountain. As soon as that second pool fills up, it too overflows…into another one farther down the slope…and another…and another…until the last and final pool pours its contents into the immensity of God's sea.

As I stood with my family looking at this wondrous handiwork of God, I thought about how these seven pools illustrate for us the fullness we can enjoy—and the far-reaching impact we can have—as we live according to God's plan.

Picture again that top pool, high on that mountain.

Like that initial pool, veiled in a cloudy mist and hidden from the sight of others, you and I enjoy our hidden life with God, the private life we nurture in Him. When we are filled with His goodness, that fullness overflows down into the next pool, the heart of the person nearest and dearest to us—our husband. Then it happens again...

This crystal pool of loving service swells until it cascades into the hearts of our children, refreshing and supplying their tender hearts and filling our home with God's love and the beauty of family. Soon, too, this pool is filled to overflowing...

And then the waters rush down to the next level where dreams are dreamed, where we get a glimpse of what God wants you and me to do for Him and His people. As we submerge ourselves in this fresh pool of knowledge, discipline, and training, sure enough, the water level rises to the brink and surges beyond its limits, pouring forth into God's limitless ocean of ministry.

Beloved, when you and I are faithful to follow after God's heart—when we tend and nurture each aspect of life as He instructs—the ministry He uses us in can have an impact beyond measure!

*Father of all love...*
*Thank You for Your plan for my life.*
*May my life be filled and overflowing with Your love.*
*Thank You that every good deed done in Your power*
*produces ministry beyond measure.*

# How a Garden Grows

*And we pray...*
*that you may live a life worthy of the Lord*
*and may please him in every way:*
*bearing fruit in every good work,*
*growing in the knowledge of God.*

—COLOSSIANS 1:10

$\mathcal{I}$ wish you could see my friend Judy's lovely and serene country garden. Over the past few years, she has added much for her visitors to ooh and aah over. One of those additions is the arbor which her white iceberg roses have claimed as their own.

Whenever I stand on Judy's porch, my eye travels first to that sweet arbor, a quaint reminder of times gone by. The urge to stroll down the pressed gravel path that passes through its magical opening is irresistible! A delight to the senses, this gracious rose arbor provides gentle fragrance, cool shade, and refreshing beauty—and I'm never alone as I approach. Birds, butterflies, and the neighbor's cat are also drawn there. All creatures—great and small—love Judy's rose arbor.

Needless to say, something this lovely is certainly no accident, and it didn't happen instantaneously. Much time and attention went into creating this lovely garden retreat, and the time and effort continue. Judy works hard tending her arbor, first faithfully feeding and tilling and watering it in the cool early-morning stillness. Then, retrieving her sharpened shears from the storage shed, Judy begins the painstaking routine of cutting away unruly growth, pruning off unnecessary shoots, and removing dead blossoms. Performing this surgery—removing anything that would hinder the formation and development of her roses—is a crucial task. The meticulous training still remains to be done, and Judy does this by tacking down and wiring her roses, interweaving the loose branches and blooms, carefully directing and redirecting their growth. People enjoy a place of great beauty because of Judy's labor of love.

Like Judy's garden, you and I enjoy beauty in our life when we work in the same diligent and deliberate way. As we pare away the actions and habits that are unnecessary in our lives and turn our focus to what is holy and worthwhile, the thriving beauty of our faith becomes an example of God's goodness. That's how a "garden of God's grace" is grown.

*Father of all grace...*
*Thank You for the beauty of a carefully tended garden.*
*May my life display*
*the grace of Your presence,*
*the vitality of a vibrant walk with You, and*
*the health of a spiritually strong woman of faith.*

Judy Buswell
© 1995

# The Radiance of Faithfulness

*Your beauty should not come from outward adornment…*
*Instead, it should be that of your inner self,*
*the unfading beauty of a gentle and quiet spirit,*
*which is of great worth in God's sight.*

—1 PETER 3:3-4

*M*ary Jane is the pianist at my church, and I've been privileged to not only listen to Mary Jane play the piano for 27 years, but also to watch her life. You see, Mary Jane's "place" during our worship service is on the platform. It's a large platform, and very public—*right up there* in front of everyone and *right out there* under blazing lights. And there Mary Jane sits. That's her place.

And yet I have to tell you that I almost don't even notice Mary Jane. (And, as you'll soon see, that's a compliment to her!) Why? Because Mary Jane is serving the Lord. She's not performing. Mary Jane is herself worshiping the Lord. She is "performing" her service unto the Lord. And she's in His presence. She knows that, and somehow we in the congregation know that too. Her behavior is sacred because her role is sacred and her worship is sacred.

For years (because I'd never met her) I never heard Mary Jane say a word. And there are a few other *nevers* to go along with that one. In 27 years of seeing her on the platform, I've never seen her make a "grand" entrance, although she ascends and descends the steps on the worship platform every week. Because of her own state and because of the solemnness of the occasion of the worship service, I hardly notice Mary Jane.

And then one day I met Mary Jane. I now know her fairly well. And guess what? Everything about her private life fits with the image I see in public. She's a lady. She's gracious. She's concerned about others. She's confident in a good way, in the Lord, and in the roles He has given her at home and at church and with the little ones she teaches at school. Of course she's fun and fun to be with, but there's a quiet seriousness about her, a settled seriousness about who she is (she's a child of God) and what she does with her life (she serves Him in everything she does).

I thank God regularly (and certainly every Sunday) for Mary Jane. In her He has given me a living, flesh-and-blood woman who shows me many ways to faithfully answer God's high calling to godliness, and to behavior and conduct that honors Him and represents Him well.

*Father ever faithful...*
*Thank You that You care more about godliness than good looks.*
*May I be faithful to worship You in spirit and in truth,*
*to represent You in an honorable way.*

# A Legacy of Love

*Jesus...went around doing good.*

—ACTS 10:38

Our family has been most blessed by Jim's mother. You should hear Jim's list of the many "little things" dear Lois did for him! Honestly, she made being his wife hard for me. Why? Because she loved her kitchen and loved filling up Jim and his dad with her homemade delicacies.

And she loved to wash, delighting in scrubbing every spot out of every garment that her two "men" would be wearing. And that delight extended itself to her love of ironing—which extended itself to ironing Jim's sheets...and even his underwear! (Now do you see why it was a little hard for me—who was clueless—to come along behind her as Jim's caregiver?!) But seriously, Jim's mother was a saint! He has a lifetime of vivid and warm memories that center on his childhood home.

Lois's love found its ultimate expression in her own home to those most dear to her. And, as is always true of any vessel that is full, her kindness overflowed to her neighbors, those at her church and in her community— even to many missionaries around the world. Later, as a widow, Lois gave up her home and moved to be close to Jim and his family...to minister her loving-kindness to us. And, once again, those at church received the overflow of her goodness, as she drove other widows to church, prepared meals, and encouraged others verbally as well as gave to them monetarily. No price can be put on the legacy of love Lois left behind.

Yes, these are "little things," but they are priceless gifts of kindness and goodness offered up by just one little godly girl...who grew up and became one little godly wife...who became one little godly mother...who became one little godly mother-in-law...who became one little godly grandmother...who became one little godly widow...who became one little godly saint whose impact was so far-reaching that our church's chapel was filled for her memorial service with those who gave testimony of her many "little" godly deeds.

I pray that this pattern of a godly life spent in godly goodness will be true of me as well. And I pray the same for you, dear one.

*Father of all "little things"...*
*Thank You for the magnitude of Your unspeakable gift*
*of salvation and eternal life.*
*Help me to extend the gift of Your love to others*
*through a multitude of "little things."*

# Encouraging Words for Your Soul

*As the deer pants for streams of water,*

*so my soul pants for you, O God.*

*My soul thirsts for God,*

*for the living God.*

—PSALM 42:1-2

# Spiritual Refreshment

*As newborn babes,*
*desire the pure milk of the word,*
*that you may grow....*

—1 PETER 2:2 (NKJV)

One Sunday morning, I stopped on the church patio to talk to a long-time acquaintance. For the 23 years I've been at the church, Sharon has helped women like me grow in the things of the Lord and live out His priorities. Sharon has been a faithful older woman and a blessing to many.

As we talked that morning, she seemed electric—lighted up, sparks flying, flowing and sizzling with live juice. Everything about Sharon that day evidenced both the vital life she lives in the Savior and her wholehearted pursuit of continued growth in Him. I can still picture her broad, brilliant smile and her eyes bright with an inner energy. Uncontainably excited, she involuntarily punctuated her message with gestures and waves.

What was she so excited about? Well, Sharon was looking forward to hearing a very special speaker the next day. She could hardly wait, and judging by her exhilaration, I bet she didn't sleep that night! Her words tumbled out as she explained that she had already attended a weekend workshop led by this gentleman and that it had been the most exciting weekend of her life, the most stimulating thing she'd ever done. This teacher had taken Sharon to new depths in God's Word, in her understanding of His ways, and in her ministry. As she talked, I knew I was in the presence of a woman who was growing in both the knowledge and love of her Lord. No wonder she was so happy and excited! No wonder she had so much to give to others! No wonder I felt blessed by her ministry of spiritual refreshment.

*Father of all spiritual life…*
*Thank You for those who pass Your Word on to others.*
*May I grow to join their ranks.*
*May my passion for You*
*light a fire in the hearts and souls of others.*

Judy Buswell
© '95

# God's Holy Presence

*One thing I ask of the LORD...*
*that I may dwell in the house of the LORD*
*all the days of my life,*
*to gaze upon the beauty of the LORD.*

—PSALM 27:4

*W*hat a treat I savored this past spring when I
traveled with my husband Jim to England to
attend our church's European missions conference! And
one particular day turned out to be life-changing for me.
You see, our host arranged an outing for our group to the
legendary Canterbury Cathedral in Kent, England. The
area of Kent has a rich Christian history, dating back to
A.D. 597, to the days of Saint Augustine, and the
Canterbury Cathedral there is heralded as one of the finest
ecclesiastical structures in England. I've never seen anything so magnificent.

Anyway, while Jim and I were walking through the 80-
foot-high stone porticos of the cathedral and sitting in its
centuries-old pews in order to take in the lofty archways,
towering columns, and ornate ceilings, we became quietly
aware of the clergy who tended to the church and the
people who worshiped there. They moved about silently—
so silently that we were never distracted. They moved
reverently—never for a second forgetting that they were in
a place of worship. They spoke little, if at all, and always in

quiet tones. One could almost sense their awareness that they were in the presence of God.

Everything about our visit to the Canterbury Cathedral was spiritually uplifting. Why? Well, certainly the majestic architecture contributed to our experience. But more than the *place*, the *people* there who served and worshiped with reverence inspired the same in us. Suddenly we found ourselves whispering. Why? They were quiet…therefore we were quiet. Without our noticing, our breakneck tourist pace slowed to a stroll. Why? Because they were moving silently, reverently, worshipfully…therefore we did too. One couldn't help but pray in such a place. Again, why? Because the church attendants seemed to be absorbed in worship and in the God they served…therefore we were too.

All this reminded both Jim and me that we were not in a museum or a well-preserved architectural model. No, as I said, we were in a place of worship. And somehow, the reverential behavior of others brought to us a fresh awareness of God's holy presence. We'll never forget that wonderful spring afternoon in England!

*Father who art holy, holy, holy…*
*Thank You that I may enjoy Your presence*
*through Your Son, Jesus Christ.*
*May my behavior reflect Your presence and*
*may Your presence affect my behavior.*

# Tending Your Spiritual Roots

*Blessed is the man [whose]...*
*delight is in the law of the LORD...*
*He is like a tree planted by streams of water,*
*which yields its fruit in season*
*and whose leaf does not wither.*

—PSALM 1:1-3

The Bible speaks of "a time to plant," and for my husband Jim that time came as a result of the massive 1994 earthquake that occurred while we were living in Southern California. A part of the devastation we

experienced at our home (only three miles from the quake's epicenter) was the loss of our block wall fences.

After a year of waving to our neighbors only a few feet away, it was a blessing to have those fences back in place. But the new walls were so bleak! So naked! The old ones had been charming—seasoned by age, blanketed by climbing roses and ivy, serving as friendly arms that embraced our lawn, patio, house, and anyone who happened to be there enjoying the beauty. And now we were forced to start all over again. It was our time to plant!

So Jim planted…13 baby creeping figs whose job it was to soften the harshness of the new walls. Twelve of those new figs dutifully shot out their magic fingers and began a friendly possession of the wall. One plant, however, slowly withered, shrank, dried up, and finally died.

Coming home from work on a Friday afternoon, Jim picked up a replacement plant at the nursery, changed clothes, got out our shovel, and bent over the dead vine, fully prepared to work at digging it out of the ground so he could put the new one in. But much to his surprise, the shovel wasn't necessary. As he grasped the plant, it easily came out of the ground. There were no roots! Although the plant had enjoyed all the right conditions above ground, something was missing beneath the surface of the soil. It didn't have the root system vital for drawing the needed nourishment and moisture from the soil.

This garden scenario portrays a spiritual truth for you and me as God grows in us a heart of faith—we must be devoted to nurturing a root system. Roots make all the difference in the health of a plant, and their presence or absence ultimately becomes known to all. The plant either flourishes or fails, thrives or dies, blossoms or withers. The health of anything—whether a garden plant or a heart devoted to God—reflects what is going on (or not going on!) underground.

What are you doing to care for your spiritual roots?

*Father of all grace and knowledge...*
*Thank You for the fruit You bear*
*in those whose roots are grounded in the truth.*
*May I delight in tending to my spiritual growth*
*so that I may flourish...even in dry and difficult times!*

# The Great Exchange

*Trust in the LORD with all your heart*
*and lean not on your own understanding;*
*in all your ways acknowledge him,*
*and he will make your paths straight.*

—PROVERBS 3:5-6

*I*f you want—or need—to be encouraged, then make
time to spend time with God. Why? Because when
you and I do slip away to be with God in study and prayer,
we receive. We take in. We are nurtured and fed. We

insure our spiritual health and growth. When we spend time with the Lord, He supplies us with strength and encourages us in the pursuit of His ways.

I call this time with God "the great exchange." Away from the world and hidden from public view, I exchange my weariness for His strength, my weakness for His power, my problems for His solutions, my frustrations for His peace, and the impossible for the possible!

I saw the reality of this great exchange at our church's annual women's retreat. My roommate and dear friend was in charge of this event, attended by some 500 women. Karen handled each challenge graciously and put her administrative genius to work with each crisis. But I noticed that, as the starting time for each session neared and panic rose among the organizers who hoped things would go smoothly, Karen disappeared. As breathless, per-spiring, frazzled women came running into our room, ask-ing, "Where's Karen? We've got a problem!" she was nowhere to be found.

On one of those mysterious occasions I glimpsed Karen walking down the hotel hall with her retreat folder and burgundy Bible in hand. She had carefully gone over the plans, the schedule, and the announcements one last time. But she sensed a need for one more thing—quiet time with God alone. She needed to look at a few precious portions of His empowering Word and then place our event completely in God's hands through prayer.

Later—after Karen reappeared from her time of taking in—I couldn't help but notice the sharp contrast between her and the others. As the anxiety of other women rose, Karen exhibited God's perfect peace. As they fretted, worried, and wondered, Karen knew all was and would be well. As others wilted under the pressure, Karen's strength—God's strength in Karen—shone with a supernatural brilliance. Underground and away from the crowd, she had exchanged her needs for God's supply.

Now, do you need encouragement? Then seek the Lord...and the power of His might! Spend some time with Him.

*Father of all compassion...*
*Thank You that You encourage me in all my troubles.*
*May I remember to look to You*
*for my every need and*
*exchange my cares for Your comfort.*

# Trust and Obey

*Delight yourself in the LORD*
*and he will give you the desires of your heart.*
*Commit your way to the LORD;*
*trust in him and he will do this.*

—PSALM 37:4-5

One evening as I was reading, I was struck by an account of a woman who seriously wanted to be God's kind of woman. Her name was Irene, and she was a Bible teacher much in demand. Her husband Mike, however, was a nominal Christian who went to church but didn't get any more involved than that. Irene's priority list looked like this: #1) God, #2) Teaching women's Bible studies, and #3) Family.

One day the Lord spoke to Irene through a verse in Ephesians: "Wives be subject—be submissive and adapt yourselves—to your own husband as (a service) to the Lord" (5:22).[1] When she saw this familiar verse in a different translation, Irene realized that serving her husband was a ministry, a service to the Lord. She began to seriously evaluate her life and her priorities.

Did she really love Mike? Did she put him first? She was everything to the Christian community she served, but not everything to Mike.

After much prayer, Irene decided to drop her outside activities and began to spend more time with Mike. When the church asked her to teach, she declined. When a friend asked her to lead a home Bible study, she refused. She stayed home with Mike. She watched TV with him, jogged with him, played cribbage, and made love to him. Irene dropped out of the picture as far as a visible Christian ministry was concerned.

The subsequent two years were painful, like "walking in a dark valley." Mike continued as a so-so Christian. Then in the middle of the third year, something stirred in Mike. He began to lead devotions and to do some teaching. His commitment to Christ solidified and God began to develop him into a Christian leader. Irene realized that if she had remained in the limelight, Mike would have been too threatened to venture out. Today, at Mike's insistence, they together teach a class for couples.[2]

As this faithful woman trusted God and obeyed His Word, God changed her heart...and her life! And He can do the same for you when you trust and obey.

*Father of all blessings...*
*Truly, Your ways are not my ways.*
*Grow in me a heart of trusting obedience.*
*Help me to want what You want*
*more than what I want.*

# Cultivating a Heart of Prayer

*And pray in the Spirit on all occasions*
*with all kinds of prayers and requests.*

—EPHESIANS 6:18

*I* remember one particularly special day very clearly. It was my tenth spiritual birthday and a significant turning point for me.

Having dropped my two daughters off at school and

gotten my husband Jim off to work, I sat at my desk in the family room, alone in the house with only the sound of our wall clock ticking. Resting there before God and rejoicing in a decade of being His child, I thought back over those ten years. Although at times they'd been rough, God's great mercy, His wisdom in every circumstance, and His care in leading and keeping me were all very obvious.

Overwhelmed with gratitude, I lifted my heart and prayed, "Lord, what do You see missing from my Christian life? What needs attention as I begin a new decade with You?" God seemed to respond immediately by calling to my mind an area of great personal struggle and failure—my prayer life.

Oh, I had tried praying. But each new effort lasted, at best, only a few days. I would set aside time for God, read my Bible, and then dutifully bow my head, only to mumble a few general words which basically added up to "God, please bless me and my family today." Certainly God intended prayer to be more than that—but I couldn't seem to do it.

But on that spiritual birthday I reached for a small book of blank pages that my daughter Katherine had given me for Mother's Day four months earlier. It had sat unused on the coffee table because I hadn't quite known what to do with it. But suddenly I knew exactly how to put it to use. Full of resolve, conviction, and desire, I wrote these words—straight from my heart—on the first page: "I dedicate and purpose to spend the next ten years (Lord willing) developing a meaningful prayer life."

These are simple words, written and prayed from a

simple desire within my heart. But that day, those simple words, and that little blank book began for me an exciting leg on my adventure of following after God's own heart. My new commitment to prayer put into motion a complete makeover of my life—every part and person and pursuit in it. I fully expected drudgery and joyless labor, but as I moved ahead on my commitment to cultivate a heart of prayer, I was surprised by the blessings that began to blossom in my heart. As a favorite hymn tells you and me, "Count your blessings, name them one by one." And the result? "And it will surprise you what the Lord hath done."

*Father of answered prayer...*
*I praise You that I can call upon You.*
*May my prayers echo Your heart,*
*May my desires reflect Your will.*

# Encouraging Words for Your Home

*The wise woman builds her house.*

*She watches carefully all that goes on*

*throughout her household.*

—PROVERBS 14:1 AND 31:27 (TLB)

# Becoming a Helper

*The LORD God said, "It is not good for the man to be alone.*
*I will make a helper suitable for him."*

—GENESIS 2:18

*I*t was a bright autumn day at the University of Oklahoma. As I hurried toward my first class after lunch, I noticed him again. Every Monday, Wednesday, and Friday our paths seemed to cross as he, too, rushed to class. His name—Jim George—was unknown to me at the time, but he looked extremely nice, he was cute, and I loved his smile! Well, evidently he noticed me too, because soon a mutual friend introduced us.

That was in November, 1964. On Valentine's Day we were engaged, and our wedding took place the first weekend school was out, June 1, 1965. That was 35 years ago—and I wish I could say, "That was 35 wonderful, blissful, happy years ago," but I can't. You see, Jim and I began our marriage without God, and that meant rough times. From the beginning we fumbled, we argued, and we let each other down. Because we didn't find fulfillment in our marriage, we poured our lives into causes, friends, hobbies, and intellectual pursuits. Having two children also didn't fill the emptiness we each felt. Our married life droned on for eight frustrating years until, by an act of God's grace, we became a Christian family, a family centered on Jesus Christ as the head, a family with the Bible to guide us.

I had much to learn about being a woman, a wife, a mother who pleased God, and as I began reading through the Bible, God went to work on my makeover. Soon I came across the first aspect of my job assignment as a Christian wife—I was to serve Jim. I marked these words in my Bible, "It is not good that man should be alone; I will make him a helper comparable to him" (Genesis 2:18 NKJV). From that day until now I ask Jim these two questions every morning—

—What can I do for you today?
—How can I help you make better use of your time today?

I want to become a better helper. How about you?

*Father of all creation...*
*Thank You for my exalted role of "helper."*
*May I follow in Your Son's sacred footsteps,*
*who came to serve...not to be served.*

# Loving Your VIPs

*The younger women [are] to love their…children.*

—TITUS 2:4

*L*ate one afternoon I was hurrying my two little girls into the car so we could deliver a meal to "Mrs. X" who had just had a baby. All day long I'd labored on the meal for this woman who needed the help of people in the church, a woman I didn't even know. I had baked a pink, juicy ham, created a pressed Jello® salad in a pretty mold, steamed brightly colored vegetables, and topped it all off with my most special dessert. As we started out the front door, Katherine and Courtney wanted to know who the food was for. I lowered the beautifully arranged tray to their level and took advantage of this opportunity to teach them about Christian giving. I explained, "Mrs. X has had a baby and we're taking dinner to her family so she can rest after being in the hospital."

That sounded good...until my own children asked, "What are we having for dinner?" When I said that we were having macaroni and cheese with hot dogs (again!), I was sharply convicted of my wrong priorities. I had put someone else, Mrs. X, ahead of my own family. I had gone many extra miles to make the meal I was taking to someone I had never met, but I was throwing together something quick and easy for my own husband and children, my God-given VIPs. In short, I was giving something to someone else that I had not first given to the people closest to me. I was failing to honor my family first.

Since that moment, I have made the same meal for my own precious ones—people light-years more precious to me than anyone else ever will be—that I make when I do a good deed. And when I take a dish to a potluck, I make two of them. When I take a dessert for some gathering, I take it with two or three pieces missing—pieces left behind for my VIPs, proof of my love for them, proof of their place of preference in my heart.

To whom are you showing preference?

*Father who art in heaven...*

*Your Son Jesus took time to*

*bless the little ones who came to Him.*

*May I demonstrate such a heart of love to my VIPs.*

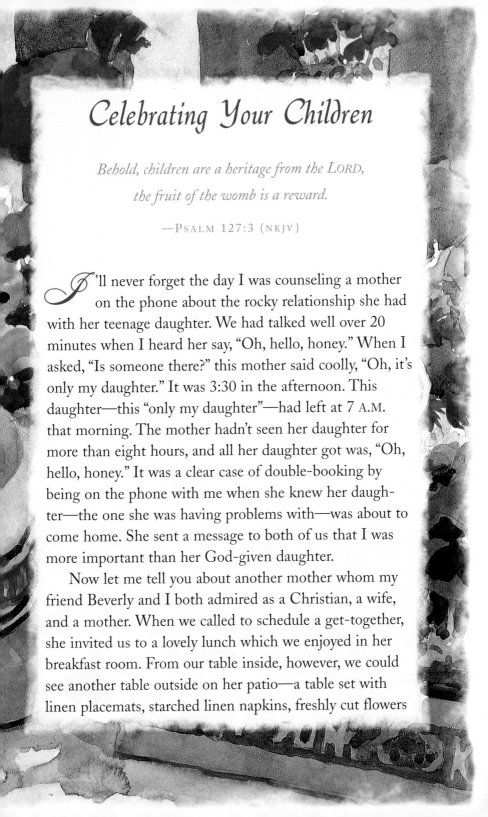

# Celebrating Your Children

*Behold, children are a heritage from the LORD,*
*the fruit of the womb is a reward.*

—PSALM 127:3 (NKJV)

*I*'ll never forget the day I was counseling a mother
on the phone about the rocky relationship she had
with her teenage daughter. We had talked well over 20
minutes when I heard her say, "Oh, hello, honey." When I
asked, "Is someone there?" this mother said coolly, "Oh, it's
only my daughter." It was 3:30 in the afternoon. This
daughter—this "only my daughter"—had left at 7 A.M.
that morning. The mother hadn't seen her daughter for
more than eight hours, and all her daughter got was, "Oh,
hello, honey." It was a clear case of double-booking by
being on the phone with me when she knew her daughter—the one she was having problems with—was about to
come home. She sent a message to both of us that I was
more important than her God-given daughter.

Now let me tell you about another mother whom my
friend Beverly and I both admired as a Christian, a wife,
and a mother. When we called to schedule a get-together,
she invited us to a lovely lunch which we enjoyed in her
breakfast room. From our table inside, however, we could
see another table outside on her patio—a table set with
linen placemats, starched linen napkins, freshly cut flowers

in a vase, two sterling silver spoons, two crystal plates, and two crystal goblets for ice water. That lovely table had been set in honor of her teenage daughter's much-anticipated arrival home from school. This thoughtful, loving mom had two more desserts in long-stemmed crystal glasses waiting in the refrigerator—and she did something like this every day! And on those days when she had to be gone when her daughter came home, she left a love note on a set table and a special treat in the refrigerator.

At 2:30, this wise mother—a mother who understood her priorities—began to shoo the two of us out the door because someone more special was coming. She graciously said, "Well, I'm sorry we have to end this, but I'm expecting my daughter home in 15 minutes, and that's our special time." She was not about to lose one second of her precious time with her daughter by double-booking and having us there too! She had given us the gift of time—rich, life-changing time for Beverly and me—but our hostess truly lived out her priorities. She knew where to focus her efforts.

Now, how will you celebrate your children today?

*Father of all blessings...*
*Thank You for the gift of children—*
*both mine and others.*
*Fill me with Your love and joy*
*as I celebrate, serve, and train them for You.*

# Kind Words
# to Nurture the Heart

*She speaks with wisdom,*
*and faithful instruction is on her tongue.*

—PROVERBS 31:26

*O*ne day a friend of mine communicated volumes about her home life (and her heart) as she warned a group of younger moms, "Just you wait! Having teenagers is awful!"

How I thank God for Betty, a sharp contrast to my friend. Betty never failed to speak positively and enthusiastically about her child-raising years. She would ask me, "How old are the girls now?" When I answered, "Nine and ten," she exclaimed, "Oh, I remember when my boys were nine and ten! Those were wonderful years!" Years later when my answer to her same question was "Thirteen and fourteen," Betty again cried out, "Oh, I remember when my boys were thirteen and fourteen! Those were wonderful years!" No matter what age Katherine and Courtney were, Betty saw them as wonderful years. Oh, I'm sure she encountered the usual challenges, but Betty was a mother whose heart was filled with motherly affection for her boys, whose home was filled with fun, whose heart was positive about God's job assignment for her—and whose lips were respectfully quiet about any difficulties.

One of God's solutions for the challenges we face raising children (the children He gives us and the challenges He knows we face as we train them up) is the "older women" at church. So I encourage you to develop a relationship with a woman a little older than you, a woman like Betty who can help and encourage you. Talk to her—and to God—about mothering. Ask her and the Lord your questions about how to fulfill that awesome responsibility and blessed privilege with a heart of affection for your children.

And what if you are a little older yourself? Please, own your role as an "older woman." Pass on what you now know. Share your wisdom. Let your kind words nurture and encourage the heart of a struggling young mom.

*Father of all wisdom…*
*Grant that my words may be*
*filled with Your wisdom and kindness.*
*Help me to pass Your goodness along to others,*
*to speak gracious words of instruction to hurting hearts.*

# A Sanctuary Called Home

*By wisdom a house is built,*
*and through understanding it is established;*
*through knowledge its rooms are filled*
*with rare and beautiful treasures.*

—PROVERBS 24:3-4

*O*ne evening at bedtime, right before I turned off my light, I read this lovely description of a home written by Peter Marshall, former chaplain of the United States Senate. Maybe it will open your eyes and touch your heart as it did mine.

*I was privileged, in the spring, to visit in a home that was to me—and I am sure to the occupants—a little bit of Heaven.*

*There was beauty there. There was a keen appreciation of the finer things of life, and an atmosphere in which it was impossible to keep from thinking of God.*

*The room was bright and white and clean, as well as cozy. There were many windows. Flowers were blooming in pots and vases, adding their fragrance and beauty. Books lined one wall—good books—inspiring and instructive—good books—good friends. Three bird cages hung in the brightness and color of this beautiful sanctuary, and the songsters voiced their appreciation by singing as if their little throats would burst.*

*Nature's music, nature's beauty—nature's peace....It seemed to me a kind of Paradise that had wandered down, an enchanted oasis—home.[3]*

What hit me—aside from the beauty of this image—was the realization that my home (and yours) can be a little bit of heaven, a kind of paradise, to my dear family and to all who enter its sanctuary. As I fell asleep that night, I dreamed about making my house a place of beauty, a sanctuary, a home in which it was impossible to keep from thinking of God.

I'm sure you have the same dream.

*Father of all beauty…*
*Thank You for Your promise of a home in Heaven.*
*While I wait for Paradise,*
*may I make my home on earth*
*a little bit of Heaven on earth.*

# Longing for Home

*We have a building from God,*
*an eternal house in heaven,*
*not built by human hands.*

—2 CORINTHIANS 5:1

s the center of family life, the home ministers to our family far more than we might imagine. I remember a time my husband made this fact very clear. He'd had "one of those days" that had stretched him to his absolute limit. A seminary student at the time, Jim had left the church parking lot at 5:00 A.M. to attend classes and deliver his senior sermon. After his commute back to the church through downtown Los Angeles traffic, he had officiated at a funeral and graveside service for a woman who, having no one to help bury her husband, had called the church the day Jim was "pastor of the day." All of this was topped off with a late meeting at church.

I had the porch light on and was watching out the kitchen window as I waited for Jim. When he finally got to the front door, he didn't walk in—he sort of slumped in, half falling as I opened the door. On the way in, my exhausted husband sighed, "All day long I kept telling myself, 'If I can just get home, everything will be all right.'"

"If I can just get home, everything will be all right." What a blessing it would be if every member of your family and mine knew that there is one place on earth where everything will be all right! Home would truly be a wonderful haven and refuge for them, a hospital. And what a worthwhile goal for us—to build the kind of home which strengthens and renews each family member. Mrs. Dwight Eisenhower had that goal for her famous husband and president of the United States: She wanted to build home where he "belonged to her world, a world of light-hearted family life where there were no pressures."[4] Imagine such a refuge!

Beloved, everyone longs for "home"—both an eternal home in heaven as well as a physical home on earth. Won't you put forth the effort, open up your heart and your home, and extend a little bit of heaven on earth to your friends and loved ones?

*Father of all protection...*
*Thank You for the privilege of being a home-maker.*
*May the home I build serve others as a refuge of strength*
*and a place of safety in times of trouble.*

# Home Management—
# God's Way!

*She watches carefully*
*all that goes on throughout her household,*
*and is never lazy.*

—PROVERBS 31:27 (TLB)

hink for a moment about the feeling you get when you enter a hotel room. What greets you? Order. Quiet. Cleanliness. You can still see the vacuum tracks in the carpet. The bed is made. The first sheet of toilet paper has been folded to a point. No TV or stereo is blaring.

Order reigns. Someone has done the work of effective management, and their efforts make the room a sanctuary.

One day Jim and I checked out of just such a place. We had been staying in a hotel for six days while Jim was processed at Los Alamitos Army Headquarters for five months of active duty. Jim is in the ministry, but he has been a pharmacy officer in the U.S. Army Reserves since college. This was our first time for activation and deployment in over thirty years. Well, Los Alamitos was too far from our home for Jim to commute back and forth for six days. Hence, the hotel stay. And the entire time we were there, I had that feeling of order despite the fact it was a time of great chaos for our family.

When we checked out, the hotel clerk gave me a card to fill out, rating the facilities and the service we had received during our stay. It was a pleasure to give a top rating on every count. We had been well taken care of. The hotel staff met our needs as they took care of our room and our food, even giving me a 30% discount on meals!

As I filled out that evaluation card, I wondered how the Lord—and my family—would rate my service, my meals, and my management. With the Lord's grace and with management skills I've learned and practiced over the years, I'm doing better. God's ways work!

*Father of all order…*
*Your ways are perfect, dependable, and unchanging.*
*Create in me a desire to work hard, follow Your instructions,*
*and faithfully carry out my responsibilities at home.*

# Weaving a Tapestry of Beauty

*She…works with eager hands.*

—PROVERBS 31:13

Jane is an amazing woman, clearly a woman after God's own heart. Although we are the same age, she seems to possess the wisdom of a woman a quarter of a century older than me. As I watched her, I saw a godliness that spoke of her carefully nurtured relationship with God. When I saw Jane with her husband, I saw a woman who helped, respected, and loved her husband. And her

two pre-school age boys were obedient, polite, and definitely under control!

Finally I found the courage to call Jane and ask to meet with her. She was absolutely delighted (I could hear it in her voice). And do you know where she wanted to meet? In her home where—like its mistress—everything was clean, neat, efficient, tidy, and in order. (Notice that I didn't say "a large, gorgeous showplace.")

I praise the Lord that Jane spent that time with me because she gave me the initial direction and nudge for me to tackle weaving my own tapestry of beauty, my tapestry of home. We first talked at length about her devotional life. Besides telling me exactly what she studied and how she did it, she showed me where she studied and let me peek at her prayer journal.

Then we talked about marriage. She suggested a list of the best books to read and, again, shared with me exactly how she tried to love and serve her husband. The same with her sons. Jane made me privy to her personal and biblical principles for discipline, training, and love in the home.

Finally we got to the matter of the home itself, and I really got a bonus. Jane took me on a tour of her little house, opening cupboards, drawers, closets, and doors. I was speechless. The insides of her house certainly didn't look like the insides of mine! And don't get me wrong. Jane wasn't bragging or boasting. She was teaching. She was showing me a system that worked for her. She showed me how she took care of her home in a minimum of time.

You can't put a price on a lesson like that! I got it all, I heard it all, and I saw it all. Those few hours with Jane were definitely life-changing.

*Father of all glory and Designer of all creation…*
*May my efforts at home and my labors of love*
*produce a tapestry of beauty—*
*a home that blesses all who enter and blazes forth Your glory.*

# Notes

1. *The Amplified Bible* (Grand Rapids, MI: Zondervan Bible Publishers, 1965), p. 302.
2. Drawn from Pat King, *How Do You Find the Time?* (Edmonds, WA: Aglow Publications, 1975), page unknown.
3. Catherine Marshall, *A Man Called Peter* (New York: McGraw-Hill, 1961), p. 65.
4. Julie Nixon Eisenhower, *Special People* (New York: Ballantine Books, 1977), p. 209.